ACTIVATING the POWER | of the CROSS

TONY EVANS

MOODY PUBLISHERS

CHICAGO

© 2013 by
ANTHONY T. EVANS

All rights reserved. No part of this book may be reproduced in any form without permission in writing from the publisher, except in the case of brief quotations embodied in critical articles or reviews.

All Scripture quotations are taken from the *New American Standard Bible*®, Copyright © 1960, 1962, 1963, 1968, 1971, 1972, 1973, 1975, 1977, 1995 by The Lockman Foundation. Used by permission. (www.Lockman.org)

Editor: Kathryn Hall
Interior Design: Ragont Design
Cover Design: Barb Fisher / LeVan Fisher Design
Cover Image: Michael D. Brown / Shutterstock Images

ISBN 978-0-8024-0722-1

We hope you enjoy this book from Moody Publishers. Our goal is to provide high-quality, thought-provoking books and products that connect truth to your real needs and challenges. For more information on other books and products written and produced from a biblical perspective, go to www.moodypublishers.com or write to:

Moody Publishers
820 N. LaSalle Boulevard
Chicago, IL 60610

Moody Publishers is committed to caring wisely for God's creation and uses recycled paper whenever possible. The paper in this book consists of 10 percent post-consumer waste.

1 3 5 7 9 10 8 6 4 2

Printed in the United States of America

CONTENTS

Introduction   5

1. The Centrality of the Cross   7

2. The Authority of the Cross   27

3. The Stability of the Cross   47

4. The Identification with the Cross   67

The Urban Alternative   85

INTRODUCTION

We live in a digital age. The technology that surrounds us enables us to experience advances and opportunities in our daily lives. Smart phones offer more than just a portal for communication. They give us the option to explore, track our fitness progress, budget our finances, get where we need to go, play games, listen to music, watch movies, and much more. Televisions introduce us to an entire world within the convenience of our own homes. Computers grant us the ability to create, write, produce, plan, design, and do any number of things.

But take a moment and imagine what our lives would be like if none of these convenient and beneficial pieces of technology were powered on. While they would still contain within them everything necessary to provide us with what we need, they would be useless. The countless hours, millions of dollars, and sheer genius that had been poured into the creation and production of these technological devices would not be leveraged to their full potential.

It would be a sheer waste.

However, there is something much more powerful than technology today which also has the potential to positively influence every aspect of your life, and yet it may frequently go inactivated. The cross is a 2,000-year-old resource that is often untapped. If you do not know how to or fail to activate the power of the cross— thereby accessing all that is contained within it and through it—then all of the benefits, blessings, and power remain dormant.

You've got to activate the power in order to experience the power.

I hope this book helps you understand and utilize the power of the cross so that you will live a life full of the victory that has been gained for you through this unique phenomenon called the cross of Jesus Christ.

1

THE CENTRALITY
OF THE CROSS

As a boy growing up in Baltimore, I had a regular Saturday regimen. First, I would finish the home responsibilities that my mom had assigned me. Then, when all of my chores were done—usually by noon—I would head down to the diamond.

The "diamond" was a large field located just a few minutes from my house where the guys gathered every Saturday to play football.

I could never get enough of football. It was my passion. Even though I played in school during the week as a halfback, and even if there was a Friday night game the evening before, you could still locate me every single Saturday at the diamond.

On one occasion, we had all gathered down at the

diamond for our Saturday afternoon game. Typically, we would play from noon until dark. As always, we had chosen sides, and then it was time for the game to commence. However, when we started to line up across from each other, everyone began to look around for the football. Unfortunately, on this particular Saturday, no one had brought a football.

While we had taken the time to go to the diamond, and while we had been proactive to choose up teams in order to begin the battle, everything came to an abrupt end simply because the football was missing in action. We were not able to do what we had gathered to do because the main thing was missing.

Isn't it amazing how something so small can carry so much weight? The people were there. The field was there. The plan was there. The spectators were there. The teams were there. Yet, because the main thing wasn't there, nothing else mattered.

We couldn't play football without the football.

You see, in the game of football—the football determines everything. First downs are measured by where the ball is placed. Touchdowns are measured by whether the ball crosses the plane. Out-of-bounds is tied to an individual's control of the ball and its relationship to the feet of the person holding it. Fumbles are determined by who grabs the ball. Field goals are measured by whether the ball goes through the uprights. All in all, men fight over it, rejoice over it, and strive to possess it.

In so many words, if a football is missing then there is

no football game. Without the football, everything else that goes on in a stadium—or on a field such as the diamond where I once played—is a waste of time.

Suffice it to say, in a football game, the football is the main thing.

Friend, I want to share something incredibly important with you: in Christianity, the cross is the main thing.

What Jesus satisfied and gained at the cross is the main thing. Without it, there is no power, no freedom, no forgiveness, no authority, no strength, no victory— nothing at all. The cross is the main thing.

> ## IF WE LEAVE OUT THE CROSS, WE ARE ONLY LEFT WITH THE EMPTY SHELL CALLED RELIGION.

Every year around Easter time, people will typically focus on the cross. We remember that Christ's death paid the penalty for our sins. We meditate on how the reality of the cross enables those who believe and trust in Jesus to spend eternity in heaven. However, once Easter passes, we frequently go back to doing our own thing and trying to live our lives without the cross of Christ as the central focus.

This makes about as much sense as if the NFL decided to supply a football for the Super Bowl only and not use any footballs for the other weeks of the season leading up to it. Without a football every week, having one at the Super Bowl isn't going to do anyone much good.

See, it isn't enough to gather together at the right place each Sunday: the church. It isn't enough to gather together with the right people in our lives: fellow believers. It isn't enough that there is a program and a plan, or that there are books, seminars, worship time on Sundays, and personal devotional time throughout the week. All of that is good, and all of that is critical. But all of that means nothing without the centrality of the main thing: the cross. If we leave out the cross, we are only left with the empty shell called religion.

We are left with an empty set of rules, laws, requirements, judgments, and all else to try and legislate spirituality without the power, intimacy, grace, and ability to live spiritually victorious lives. As a result, believer after believer finds themselves in perpetual defeat: never measuring up, never fully overcoming their struggles, never rising above their circumstances.

Sadly, many believers fail to fulfill their destiny and achieve the complete manifestation of their own significance simply because they are operating without the power and deliverance of the cross. They are trying to live the Christian life without the main thing, which makes as much sense as trying to play a football game without a football.

Oftentimes we will wear a cross around our necks. We also hang pictures, banners, and replicas of it around our homes and churches. Some even tattoo it on body parts or dangle it from their ears. Yet, in doing these things, we run the risk of denying the cross its true meaning and power. We have run the risk of belittling its authentic strength. We have turned it into an emblem, good luck charm, or decoration rather than leverage the authority and ability that the cross grants.

Essentially, we have made the cross nothing more than a replica to induce guilt rather than what it is—the single greatest affirmation and demonstration of pure love.

The problem in our personal lives, homes, churches, and communities today is not a problem of a lack of knowledge. It is not a problem of a lack of skills. It is not even entirely a problem of a lack of motivation. Many believers today want to live in victory yet continually live defeated lives.

The problem that we face in our modern, contemporary Christian culture is that we have forgotten the purpose, the preeminence, and the power of the cross. We view it as an icon reflecting something that happened thousands of years ago but has little relevance to us today.

Far too many Christians regard the cross as an historical event that will take them to heaven one day rather than as a current event wielding everything they need to bring heaven to bear on earth.

PAUL WRITES ABOUT THE CROSS

In writing to his audience at Galatia, Paul urged them over and over again, in one form or another, to remember Christ and the cross. As Paul concluded his letter to the Galatians, he did what we will often do today through the use of italics, underlining, bolding the font, or other forms of highlighting. He emphasized his point by writing largely. In essence, Paul was saying, "I don't want you to miss this part. Everything that I've said up until now has been important, but this part is the zinger. This part is what I don't want you to ever forget. Pay attention here. Read closely. Know that this is coming directly from me."

Paul wrote in "large letters" with his own hand (Galatians 6:11) in order to tell his audience that he was the one writing, and that the truth he was telling them came from one source. He wrote in verse 14, "But may it never be that I would boast, except in the cross of our Lord Jesus Christ."

Paul had been saved for some time. Yet he was still saying, "I'm only going to brag on the cross." He did not let the historical reality of the cross get lost in his mind, thoughts, function, teaching, or calling. Paul's only point of reference for his life was the cross of Christ. He wrote earlier in his letter to the Galatians a verse that we will look at more closely in the final chapter. It contains a message that ought to serve as the central point of our Christian lives,

I have been crucified with Christ; and it is no longer I who live, but Christ lives in me; and the life which I now live in the flesh I live by faith in the Son of God, who loved me and gave Himself up for me. (Galatians 2:20)

To Paul, the cross wasn't a decoration or an icon. The cross was the centrality of his very existence. The cross was the air of his every breath, the beat of his heart, and the very substance of his significance. It was the power to overcome his weaknesses. It was his identity and it was his hope.

RELIGION OR RELATIONSHIP

The reason why Paul spent so much effort focusing on the cross in his letter to the church at Galatia was because they had become confused about what true spirituality and power meant. They had begun to look to the flesh—something easy for many of us to do—instead of to the power of Christ. Paul gives us insight into their mindset when he writes,

You foolish Galatians, who has bewitched you, before whose eyes Jesus Christ was publicly portrayed as crucified? This is the only thing I want to find out from you: did you receive the Spirit by the works of the Law, or by hearing with faith? Are you so foolish? Having begun by the Spirit, are you now being perfected by the flesh? (Galatians 3:1–3)

The church members at Galatia were no longer looking to the power provided them through Christ's death
on the cross and the sending of the Holy Spirit; rather,
they were looking to themselves. They were looking to
live their lives according to what they could do instead of
what Christ already did. Paul was keenly aware of how
this mindset had crept into the hearts of the Galatians.
He reveals this to us a few chapters later when he writes,

> See with what large letters I am writing to you with
> my own hand. Those who desire to make a good
> showing in the flesh try to compel you to be circum-
> cised, simply so that they will not be persecuted for
> the cross of Christ. (Galatians 6:11–12)

Paul makes a profound statement in this verse. If you
will capture and understand it fully, it can set you on a
whole new direction for your Christian life. There was
something getting in the way of the Christians in Galatia
and hindering them from experiencing the fullness of
Jesus Christ. The thing that was keeping them from living out the blessings of the Christian experience was religion.

Religion had gotten in the way of the cross.

In that day, circumcision was the external symbol of religious commitment and involvement. In fact, there was a
specific group of people who would follow Paul around
wherever he went. Whenever he started a church, they
would try and interfere with the belief structure of the

church. This group of people was known as the "Judaizers."

The term "Judaizers" comes from the original Greek verb *ioudaïzō,* which means "live according to Jewish customs." The Judaizers were a group of people who were still attached to the religious rules of the Old Testament. Because of this, they would try and get the new Christians to conform to external religious observances, which were symbolized by the chief one known as circumcision. The Judaizers were trying to subvert the message of the cross. They had religion. They just didn't have a relationship with Jesus Christ.

However sincere it may be, whenever religious activity trumps relationship, the power of Jesus Christ is no longer experienced in the believer's life. One of the greatest dangers in our churches today is for religion to replace an intimate relationship with the Savior. By religion, I am referencing the external adherence to exercises, codes, or standards practiced in the name of God—yet apart from God.

For example, if you go to church because it is the religious, or spiritual, thing to do rather than because you are motivated to spend time worshiping God, learning about Him, and experiencing Him, then that is called religion. Religion is anything you do for God that does not stem from a heart connected to God.

One of the assignments that I had to do at seminary involved writing a research paper. I remember this particular paper because when I turned it in I was very proud of the work I had put into it. I had done my due diligence.

I had controlled the material and analyzed all of the possible idiosyncratic elements of the vicissitudes in the arguments. I felt great about my paper.

However, when I got the paper back from my professor, there was a big, fat, red zero at the top, along with a smaller note at the bottom. In a hurried hand, my professor had scrawled, "Tony, great work. Great preparation. Wrong assignment."

It wasn't that I hadn't done great work; it was that I had done my great work on the wrong assignment. I had researched the wrong topic. As a result, I didn't get credit for what I had done.

Christianity is no different. It's not that there aren't a lot of people doing a lot of excellent things. It's not that a lot of these same people attend church, help the hurting, or say all the correct spiritual platitudes. It's just that they've missed the cross. They've missed Jesus Christ. And then they wonder why they aren't getting any credit. They wonder why they aren't experiencing any victory, power, hope, and authority.

Friend, external observances—the rules of religion—can actually get in the way of a relationship. Oftentimes these religious rules are called "legalism." What legalism does is measure your spirituality by your activity. Within legalism, you must always do more, be better, go further, pray longer, and strive harder. The list goes on and on. One of the problems with legalism is that you never know when you get to the end of the list because there is always something else to add to it.

Paul wrote stern words to those contemplating following the Judaizers' path of religion in chapter five of Galatians. He said, "It was for freedom that Christ set us free; therefore keep standing firm and do not be subject again to a yoke of slavery. Behold I, Paul, say to you that if you receive circumcision, Christ will be of no benefit to you. . .You have been severed from Christ, you who are seeking to be justified by law; you have fallen from grace" (Galatians 5:1, 2, 4).

> # GOD DOESN'T WANT YOU SERVING HIM ONLY BECAUSE YOU ARE SUPPOSED TO; HE WANTS YOU SERVING HIM BECAUSE YOU LOVE HIM.

Paul uses the terms "severed from Christ" and "fallen from grace" to indicate that Jesus Christ is no longer of any benefit to you on earth. His strength, intimacy, power, and all that He has to offer have been removed from you if you are counting on yourself to be religious. The profundity of this truth is serious. What he is saying is that religious activity can actually keep Christians from experiencing the Lord. Church activity can actually keep you from Christ. Self-righteousness can keep you from true righteousness.

For example, a married woman checking off a list of things to do in her home because she is under pressure, seeking approval, or is threatened by her husband, reflects a far different relationship than a married woman who does the same list because she is motivated by love. The activity may be the same; in fact, it could be identical. But the motivation changes both the results and rewards of the activity.

One of the ways many pastors misuse and abuse their position is through preaching religion. They seek to have the pulpit control the pew through religious guilt. Such pastors turn to the Bible to make the congregation feel guilty, insisting members give more or by simply telling them they're not doing enough. But that is religion. That is legalism. That is also spiritual death.

God doesn't want you serving Him only because you are supposed to; He wants you serving Him because you love Him. He wants your morality, prayer life, dedication for Him, and all else be predicated on your relationship with Him rather than on religious duty. Instead of being defined by what you do, He wants you to be defined by who you know—Jesus Christ.

TWO CRUCIFIXIONS

Paul says there are two crucifixions that must occur on the cross in order to live a victorious Christian life:

Jesus' and your own. He emphasizes this point in the latter part of Galatians 6:14 as he writes of himself, "But may it never be that I would boast, except in the cross of our Lord Jesus Christ, through which the world has been crucified to me, and I to the world."

To identify with Jesus Christ is to identify with the cross. In other words, on the cross, Paul was crucified to all things that belong to this world. Being "crucified" with Jesus created a resultant disconnect from this world's order and subsequent attachment and alignment with Him. Paul asserts that a relationship with Christ supersedes everything this world has to offer.

The word "world" in the Greek is Kosmos. It simply refers to an organized world system or arrangement designed to promote a specific emphasis or philosophy. For example, we often talk about the "world of sports," or the "world of finance," or the "world of politics." These phrases are not referencing a location or a place. They are referencing an organized system inclusive of certain definitions, regulations, and philosophical worldviews.

When Paul states that he has been crucified with Christ, he is saying that he is no longer alive to this world's system that wants to leave God out. He refused to embrace a worldliness mentality. He was crucified to the strategies and rules that are set up to try and make humanity acceptable to God, independently of God.

I don't know if you've ever noticed, but the world does not mind religion. The world not only tolerates religion but frequently will even embrace it. Religions dominate much of humanity's systems all across the globe. However, what the world will not tolerate is the cross of Jesus Christ. As soon as you introduce Jesus into the equation, you have become too specific. Staying with references to God is okay because that can be generic and vague. But once you bring Jesus to bear on a life or a worldview, His involvement becomes too narrow for many people.

In fact, the cross is often tolerated even more so than the image of Christ on the cross. In these cases, it is merely being viewed as a religious symbol rather than as an instrument of relational sacrifice. Nonetheless, the key to the cross is not the two beams of wood, one vertical and one horizontal. The key to the cross is the One who hung on it as a sinless sacrifice.

CARRYING YOUR CROSS

Friend, the more religious you become the further from Christ you go. The cross is not about religion. It is an expression of an undying love and the payment for all of mankind's sin—past, present, and future—including yours.

Consider the harbor of a wheel. If something happens to it, the spokes become disconnected. Similarly, if you fail to make the cross the central focus of your life—your identity in Christ—you run the risk of experiencing extreme disconnection in the various areas of what you do.

Don't allow the world system that leaves God out to define you. Don't be duped into believing that you can make it by dipping in and out of both. Have you ever gone swimming in an ocean or perhaps a very deep lake? If you attempted to swim several hundred feet down in the depths of the water, you wouldn't survive simply because your body was not made for that environment. Without the proper equipment, you wouldn't last more than a few minutes.

> WE HAVE SOME MESSED-UP IDEAS ABOUT WHAT IT MEANS TO CARRY, OR BEAR, OUR CROSSES.

Friend, the cross is your equipment in this world. It is your GPS. It is your identity. It is your oxygen. It is your point of reference. It is your life. Why is it that so many believers are struggling to live victorious lives in the world? It is because they are leaving the cross at the benediction. Jesus said, "If anyone wishes to come after Me, he must deny himself, and take up his cross and follow Me" (Matthew 16:24). He didn't say that you are to pick up your cross and then set it back down. He said you are to carry your cross.

Denying oneself is a form of dying to self. It is an ongoing declaration, as Paul pointed out in his letter to the Corinthians. He said, "I affirm, brethren, by the boasting in you which I have in Christ Jesus our Lord, *I die daily"* (1 Corinthians 15:31, emphasis mine). The cross represents the moment-by-moment connection to and identification with Jesus Christ and the purpose of His life, death, burial, and resurrection. It is acknowledgment of complete and total dependency on Christ and His sufficiency, along with recognition of personal sin.

Jesus wants to be more important to you than your own comforts. Similar to Matthew, Luke also recorded Jesus' words when he wrote in chapter 14 and verse 27: "Whoever does not carry his own cross and come after Me cannot be My disciple." You must carry your cross, not Jesus' cross. He took care of His own. If you desire to follow Jesus, you need to carry your cross.

We have some messed-up ideas about what it means to carry, or bear, our crosses. A nagging physical problem, trouble with in-laws, or noisy neighbors—none of those things constitutes bearing a cross. So what does it mean to carry your cross?

Crucifixion was invented in ancient Rome. When Roman officials wanted to put a condemned criminal on public display to humiliate him, they paraded him down the street carrying the crossbeam of his cross. Carrying one's cross to the place of execution was a demonstration that the individual was guilty of the crime he was condemned for.

To carry your cross means to bear the reproach of Jesus Christ. It is to be so identified with Him that when they accuse you of being a Christian, you are found guilty.

When someone accuses you of being His disciple, you say, "You got me." In other words, to carry your own cross is to admit publicly that you are guilty of the cause of being committed to Christ, guilty of placing Him first.

What does this mean in practical terms? A young girl bears her cross when she tells her boyfriend, "I can't sleep with you because I am a Christian." It's when a businessman says, "I can't do that unethical thing. Because I am Christ's disciple, I am living by a different agenda." Carrying your cross is dying to yourself and what you want; it means putting Jesus first. It isn't comfortable to carry a cross—it takes dedication.

Religion and religious titles mean nothing. When placed against the backdrop of the cross, external paraphernalia and religious duties count for nothing. What matters is your identification with Jesus Christ and the newness of life that He brings when He lives within you. Paul tells us as he continues his letter to the Galatians, "For neither is circumcision anything, nor uncircumcision, but a new creation" (Galatians 6:15). Similarly, he writes in his letter to the Corinthians, "Therefore if anyone is in Christ, he is a new creature; the old things passed away; behold, new things have come" (2 Corinthians 5:17).

For you as a believer, victory in your daily life—decisions, emotions, finances, and in all things—completely hinges on your attachment to Jesus Christ and what He did at the cross on your behalf. It rests on His work, not on your own. It is tied to the new creation inside you, not to the flesh.

Paul concludes his letter to the believers in Galatia with this final thought. Reflecting on the fruit of living a life connected to the cross, he writes, "And those who will walk by this rule, peace and mercy be upon them, and upon the Israel of God" (Galatians 6:16).

So then, if we are connected to Him, why does God often feel so far away? It is because we are not operating by this rule. Paul says that if you walk according to the rule of the cross—that is, to align your frame of thinking, moving, and operating with the centrality of the cross— then you will experience the benefits of God. Those benefits include both peace and mercy.

On the other hand, when you are merely satisfied with religion or religious activity—or even when you have placed your trust in your religious duties to earn favor with God—you have been severed from Christ and have fallen from grace.

Falling from grace is a fairly drastic occurrence. Grace is the provision of all that you need in order to live a life of abundance and peace. To best understand what it means to be "severed from Christ" or to be "fallen from grace," I need to compare the situation to electricity. Electricity is the flow of power that makes things work in your home. Virtually everything in your house operates because of electricity. Your appliances, lights, heat, air conditioning, computers, television, and many other things work because they are receiving electricity.

If you are severed from electricity, the flow of power stops. It's not that you no longer have your possessions, nor is it that you didn't purchase them. You still own your electrical devices and appliances. But you can have something that you have paid for and not enjoy it simply because the flow of electricity is no longer there to empower it.

To be severed from Christ, or to fall from grace, means that the flow of what God wants to do in you and through you is no longer operating. You have essentially been unplugged, or disconnected, from the power of Jesus—even though you still have all of the paraphernalia of religion. Therefore, your hope is gone, your peace is gone, your courage is gone, your faith is gone, and your authority is gone.

On the other hand, those who function by the rule of the cross will experience a peace that passes understanding. The Spirit of God will permeate all that you do so much so that you begin to think differently, act differently, live differently, love differently, and even recognize yourself in a different light. You are empowered because the flow of the Spirit comes to every believer by way of the accomplishment of the cross. God will be at work in you, with you, through you, to you, and for you.

In summary, without electricity, a lot of what you own in your home would be unusable. Without a football, every game consisting of two teams with eleven men gathered on fields all over our nation would be unplayable. Electricity is essential to empowering that which was made to run on it. A football is essential to the game that was designed around it. The cross, my friend, is essential to both empowering and enabling you to live an abundant, victorious life, defined by both peace and mercy.

Never let religion get in the way of your relationship with Jesus Christ. Rather, take the cross from around your neck and carry it in your heart instead. You have been crucified with Christ—and as a result—you are a new creation.

2

THE AUTHORITY
OF THE CROSS

My calling, since I was eighteen years old, has always been to preach. Whether that means delivering God's Word at our church in Dallas on Sundays and Wednesdays, or traveling to preach in venues and churches on the road, you can find me preaching several times each week.

With such numerous travels, I have become intimately acquainted with American Airlines. That's why I wasn't surprised some time ago when I received a packet from American Airlines in the mail. This particular packet focused on the advantages that come to me as a platinum flyer. It contained a book of benefits that had accrued to me due to the large number of miles I have flown.

At first, I just tossed the booklet to the side on a stack

of papers. It didn't peak my interest right away. All that
concerned me was knowing where to board the plane and
getting to my destination. I figured what I knew in my
head was as good as what was in the packet.

> **WHAT THE CROSS PROVIDES TO YOU
> AND ME IS THE OPPORTUNITY TO SEE
> WHAT GOD CAN DO BEYOND THE
> NORMAL, EVERYDAY ROUTINE OF LIFE.**

But a few weeks later, I came across the packet again.
For some reason, this time I decided to thumb through it.
While doing so, I discovered a number of benefits that I
was not aware of. In fact, there were significant opportunities for me to take advantage of perks that I wasn't using.
There were upgrade options, booking options, and pri-
ority access options, among other things. All of these
benefits had been there for me to utilize all along. I simply did not use them because I had failed to investigate
what my relationship with the company offered.

Without fully knowing the privileges of what my platinum level relationship with American Airlines afforded
me, I failed to completely experience, realize, and maximize my "inheritance" from the airline.

It is unfortunate that many Christians come to church every Sunday and every Wednesday unaware of the rights and privileges that the cross of Christ has afforded them. They fail to maximize and utilize the benefits that God has ordained and bequeathed for His saints. Knowing about the cross without knowing the authority and benefits of the cross will keep you from experiencing all that God has in store for you.

What the cross provides to you and me is the opportunity to see what God can do beyond the normal, everyday routine of life. The cross is the key to God the Father invading the difficult or mundane circumstances of life just like He invaded the tomb of Jesus when our Lord died on the cross. Circumstances were turned around as God's power and authority was revealed.

A lot of Christians sing and talk about God's power but can never testify to experiencing divine power since they have never accessed the power of God. They have never seen Him turn, twist, and tweak things beyond their human comprehension.

Have you ever watched an action-adventure film where the hero of the story is trying to locate a special artifact or treasure? All along the way, he or she faces opposition after opposition coming from the enemy who is trying to divert the leading character from reaching his or her goal and benefiting from the prize.

These films often remind me of what Satan attempts to do in the lives of believers. See, you and I have a precious treasure, a unique possession, that our enemy doesn't want us to discover. We have benefits available to us that he doesn't want us to access. He will use no limits to stop you or me from retrieving the treasure that God has for us.

Paul gives us some insight into the benefits and authority that the treasure of the cross has to offer when he writes to the church at Ephesus. However, his letter to the Ephesians is different from many other passages. It probably wouldn't receive a passing grade in an English course.

In verses three through twelve of the first chapter, Paul writes one very long run-on sentence in the original language of Greek. It could be that he was so impassioned about what he was saying that he didn't even take the time to pause between words. Instead, he goes on, and on, and on. He just can't seem to quit.

Nevertheless, it makes sense for Paul to be beside himself concerning this topic. What he shares with the church is worthy of excitement. He tells us of the authority, benefits, and prized possessions that believers have because of the cross.

The truths present in this passage are so incredibly potent that I dare not pass over them in a summary statement. Bear with me in re-publishing the full sentence that impassioned Paul so greatly. Now with inserted sentence and paragraphs breaks having been translated into English, we read,

Blessed be the God and Father of our Lord Jesus Christ, who has blessed us with every spiritual blessing in the heavenly places in Christ, just as He chose us in Him before the foundation of the world, that we would be holy and blameless before Him.

In love He predestined us to adoption as sons through Jesus Christ to Himself, according to the kind intention of His will, to the praise of the glory of His grace, which He freely bestowed on us in the Beloved.

In Him we have redemption, through His blood, the forgiveness of our trespasses, according to the riches of His grace which He lavished on us. In all wisdom and insight He made known to us the mystery of His will, according to His kind intention which He purposed in Him with a view to an administration suitable to the fullness of the times, that is, the summing up of all things in Christ, things in the heavens and things on the earth.

In Him also we have obtained an inheritance, having been predestined according to His purpose who works all things after the counsel of His will, to the end that we who were the first to hope in Christ would be to the praise of His glory.

In Him, you also, after listening to the message of truth, the gospel of your salvation—having also believed, you were sealed in Him with the Holy Spirit of promise, who is given as a *pledge of our inheritance*, with a view to the redemption of God's own possession, to the praise of His glory.

For this reason I too, having heard of the faith in

the Lord Jesus which exists among you and your love for all the saints, do not cease giving thanks for you, while making mention of you in my prayers; that the God of our Lord Jesus Christ, the Father of glory, may give to you a spirit of wisdom and of revelation in the knowledge of Him.

I pray that the eyes of your heart may be enlightened, so that you will know what is the hope of His calling, what are the riches of the glory of His inheritance in the saints, and what is the surpassing greatness of His power toward us who believe. (Ephesians 1:3–19, emphasis mine)

As Paul reaches the end of his long, run-on sentence, he makes a pointed statement. He asks that God will open the eyes of the hearts of those to whom he is addressing his letter. Paul desires them to know what all they have gained through Christ's atonement on the cross. Similar to me not knowing what benefits I had accrued as an American Airlines platinum flyer and thus not being able to access those benefits, Paul did not want believers to go without access to the strength, power, and greatness God has in store for us.

In other words, Paul was saying that it is God's intention for you to taste of His goodness on earth before you go to heaven. He has laid up a "pledge of inheritance" for you to access right now. In Greek, the word "pledge" can mean a "down payment." Through the cross, God has set aside a "down payment" on heaven for you to receive while here on earth.

As a believer, you are on your way to heaven. However, there is no need for you to wait until you get there before you feel and experience what heaven is like. God has allocated a piece of heaven to you right now.

Are you curious what that down payment is? Or what has already been put in the will for you as a pledge of your inheritance? Paul summed it up at the end of his treatise on salvation when he said it involves, "*. . . the hope of His calling, what are the riches of the glory of His inheritance in the saints, and what is the surpassing greatness of His power. . . .*"

What I want you to notice in particular is this. He didn't write that God wants you to experience His power. Rather, he wrote that God wants you to experience the "surpassing greatness" of His power. Paul wanted you to know that God can bring blessings out of nowhere to turn things around in your life. He is the only true Super Power. No believer should ever settle for being an average individual. God has destined you for greatness through the "surpassing greatness" of His power.

SURPASSING GREATNESS

Let me give you an example of "surpassing greatness" so that you can get an idea of what it entails. Jesus was crucified and nailed to a cross on Friday. Friday was a bad day. Friday was a shameful day. Friday was a lonely day. Physically, it was a bad day because Jesus was beaten to a pulp. Emotionally, it was a bad day because Scripture says Christ cried tears of blood. Spiritually, it was a bad day because He was separated from God the Father. Friday looked like it was the last day.

> # GOD FLIPPED THE SCRIPT WITH JESUS, AND HE CAN DO THE SAME WITH YOU.

However, as bad as it was, Friday did not determine where Jesus would wind up. Paul went on to describe just what the "surpassing greatness" of God's power looks like. He summarized the almighty power of God in what happened to Jesus on the cross. He wrote,

These [the surpassing greatness of His power] are in accordance with the working of the strength of His might which He brought about in Christ, when He raised Him from the dead and seated Him at His right hand in the heavenly places, far above all rule and authority and power and dominion, and every name that is named, not only in this age but also in the one to come. (Ephesians 1:19–21)

Essentially, what started off badly on Friday wound up being divinely awesome on Sunday. This is because God reversed the effects of Friday by raising Christ from the dead and seating Him in heaven by His side.

I know that some of you reading these pages may feel beaten down or broken. Some of you may have experienced an emotional beating, a physical beating, a relational beating, or even a spiritual beating. You feel broke down—or, as we say it where I come from—tore up from the floor up. The circumstances of your life have not been in your favor.

But what I want you to know is what Paul wants you to know. That is, the surpassing greatness of God's power that worked to raise Christ from the dead, turning death into life, is the same exact surpassing greatness of power available to you today. God flipped the script with Jesus, and He can do the same with you.

Are you experiencing a deathly situation in your life? Or what feels like a crucifixion? Have you had a death in your dreams, relationships, home, career, finances, health, or in any other way? The message of the cross is that God has enough power to turn even the seemingly worst scenario into a victory—if you will just trust Him.

With the cross, we have the doctrine of the death. We also have the doctrine of the resurrection. What we often fail to appeal to and benefit from fully, however, is the doctrine of the ascension. Jesus didn't just rise from the dead. Rather, He rose and then was taken up into heaven and seated at the right hand of the Father.

While that may not sound like a lot, it is a lot. In the Old Testament days, when the priest went into the presence of God, he would find a lot of furniture inside the temple. But the one item that wasn't present was a chair. Here's the reason. The priest couldn't sit down because his work was never finished. As a result, there was no provision for him to be seated. However, when Jesus entered heaven, He was welcomed with a seat to settle in. Christ's work on earth was finished. He declared on the cross, "Tetelesti," which means, "It is finished."

But what does Jesus' dying on the cross, being raised, and then sitting down in heaven have to do with you? Everything. See, the Bible is divided into two sections: the Old Testament and the New Testament. In the old covenant found in the Old Testament, everyone was looking futuristically for God's final provision. All of the sacrifices, ceremonies, rituals, and actions were done in anticipation of God's tangible entrance into history.

Yet, for those of us who live today in the new covenant found in the New Testament, we are looking back. As a believer, you can look back to the cross as the basis for everything God has done, is doing, and will do through you and for you. It is all tied to your relationship to the cross. When you lose sight of what happened there, you can't fully experience it here. This is because if you lose sight of what Jesus accomplished on the cross, you will lose sight of your inheritance right now.

What Jesus accomplished on the cross is the gaining of the authority, benefits, and power that He now freely imparts to us. As we saw earlier, His ascension placed Him "far above all rule and authority and power and dominion, and every name that is named, not only in this age but also in the one to come" (Ephesians 1:21).

Not only did Jesus' rise to heaven place Him above all authority and power and dominion, but He also disarmed the enemies of God and sin's power over you. We read in Colossians, ". . . having canceled out the certificate of debt consisting of decrees against us, which was hostile to us; and He has taken it out of the way, having nailed it to the cross. When He had disarmed the rulers and authorities, He made a public display of them, having triumphed over them through Him" (Colossians 2:14–15).

Friend, whatever or whoever it is you are dealing with, know that it or they do not have the last say. No matter how big, mighty, powerful, or pushy they are or seem to be, know that Jesus Christ is sitting far above all of it. He is positioned higher than all rule, authority, dominion, and power.

For example, the president of the United States sits in the Oval Office at the White House. Yet, what he decrees from his position of authority can affect you wherever you are. In fact, his dictates can even impact people halfway around the world. The reason is that the president resides in a powerful location above all other powers in our nation. If one man in one city can affect an entire nation, or even the world, politically—what do you think the King of Kings and the Lord of Lords can do sitting far above all earthly rule and authority?

Consequently, whatever your enemy, opposition, circumstance, or challenge has to say is "a" word; it is not the final word. Your boss may have *a* word, but he doesn't have the final word. Your doctor may have *a* word, but he doesn't have the final word. Your finances may have *a* word, but they don't have the final word. Your emotions may have *a* word, but they don't have the final word.

What the cross accomplished for you and for me is authority. Keep in mind, authority has to do with power, but authority does not simply mean power. Authority is the right to use the power that you possess.

For example, referees are not the strongest men on the football field. In fact, they are often older, slower, and heavier. Yet, when a referee throws out a yellow flag on a player who is much bigger than him, the bigger player has to yield. The faster player has to slow down. The stronger player has to obey. This is because the referee has a greater power, called "authority." Authority overrules power.

Friend, you may be driving a bigger, more powerful vehicle than the cop car behind you, but when you see the cops' lights come on, you pull over. This is because the power of your vehicle is irrelevant in the face of authority.

Allow me to let you in on something: the Devil is bigger than you. He is more powerful than you. He is more cunning than you. He is stronger than you. You can't overrule the Devil with your human power. And I would caution you not to try. However, when you are identified with Christ—His cross, resurrection, and ascension—you are now identified with the authority that overrides Satan's power.

What Satan tries to do, however, is to get you thinking that the cross is something that belongs in the annals of history rather than in the events of today. Satan doesn't mind if you pay homage to the cross; he just doesn't want you to access the benefits and inheritance that are due you through it. That way he can continue to intimidate you with his power without you realizing that Christ's authority trumps him.

> # WHEN SATAN COMES AT YOU, REMEMBER THAT HE IS COMING AT YOU WITH AN UNLOADED GUN.

What Satan does is similar to a man holding a gun on you. At first, you may feel afraid and at the man's mercy. Yet if someone were to point out to you that the man's gun did not have any bullets in it, he would no longer control you. That's the difference between power and authority. See, at the cross, Jesus Christ "disarmed" Satan (Colossians 2:15). In other words, our Lord removed the bullets from Satan's gun.

Satan still likes to play like a tough guy and try to intimidate everyone with his power, but ultimately, our Lord has stripped him of his authority. Therefore, his power is only as strong as he can persuade you to believe that it is. In and of itself, it is not strong enough to overcome Christ's authority.

When Satan comes at you, remember that he is coming at you with an unloaded gun. Of course he's not going to tell you that. He wants you to think that you're not going to make it, that you're never going to overcome financial devastation, and that you will always be defeated. He wants you to think that since depression is in your family history, you will always fall victim to it. He wants you to think that you can never conquer negative habits, such as overspending, overeating, or other forms of addictions.

But here's the good news! Jesus wants you to know that there are no bullets in that gun! Satan was disarmed at Calvary. Satan no longer has the last word because Jesus Christ now sits high above all rule and authority.

Am I saying that you will have no problems? No. What I am saying is that if you will fix your eyes on Jesus, even though you have problems, He will teach you how to walk on water rather than drown in defeat. By His power and authority, Jesus will situate you above your circumstances rather than under them.

COMMUNION

One of the most practical ways that God has arranged for a believer to access the authority and the power of the cross on an ongoing basis is through the taking of communion. The act of communion offers more than just a physical reality. It ushers in a spiritual reality more potent than any other. Communion is the best illustration of connecting the physical with the spiritual while allowing you full entry into the accomplishments of the cross.

Communion is more than just a moment to sit quietly, think nice thoughts about Jesus, eat a wafer, and drink some juice. Communion is taking part in evoking a tremendous blessing. As Paul writes, "Is not the cup of blessing which we bless a sharing in the blood of Christ?" (1 Corinthians 10:16).

Not only is communion about reaching up into heaven to draw down the blessings attached to Christ's covenantal death and resurrection, it is also an opportunity to reach into hell to let the enemy know that he no longer holds authority over you.

BASED ON THE CUP AND THE BREAD, HELL HAS ALREADY LOST.

In the book of 1 Corinthians we read, "For as often as you eat this bread and drink the cup, you *proclaim the Lord's death* until He comes" (1 Corinthians 11:26, emphasis mine). The question coming out of this verse is: Proclaim the Lord's death to whom? And for what reason?

To proclaim something is similar to preaching it. Paul explains that when you take communion, you are preaching. *You* are preaching a sermon. And the audience to whom you are preaching your sermon is found in the book of Colossians where we read,

> When you were dead in your transgressions and the uncircumcision of your flesh, He made you alive together with Him, having forgiven us all our transgressions, having canceled out the certificate of debt consisting of decrees against us, which was hostile to us; and He has taken it out of the way, having nailed it to the cross. When He had disarmed the rulers and authorities, He made a public display of them, having triumphed over them through Him (Colossians 2:13–15).

This passage tells us what Jesus accomplished on the cross: the Devil was defeated and disarmed. He still has more power than you and I do as we looked at before, but here is the key to understanding spiritual victory in any realm. Whether it is in your relationships, your career, your emotions, or anywhere else—you must recognize that power means nothing without the authority to use it. On the cross, the Devil lost his authority. Jesus "disarmed the rulers and authorities."

Communion is your time to preach your sermon to the evil principalities and remind them that they have been defeated and that you know it. It is your turn to serve notice on hell. Based on the cup and the bread, hell has already lost.

As a believer, communion is one of the most strategic

acts of faith that you can do. When you take the bread and the blood, you can tell Satan to go to hell because it is by virtue of the bread and the blood—the body and blood of Jesus Christ—that you have the ability to piggyback on the authority of Christ over Satan.

Why do you need to serve notice on hell about your life, relationships, and all else that concerns you? It is because much of the chaos that we go through in life is coming from that realm. It is this evil spiritual realm that invades our physical realm and tries to keep us from experiencing the blessings of the sanctions of the new covenant. Therefore, you need to send a message to the enemy. Preach your sermon—faithfully and frequently.

One of the worst things you can do is to make a ritual out of what is supposed to be sacred. Don't ever allow communion, something so completely profound, to turn into something so completely ordinary. Preach, and preach truth. Serve notice that the God of the covenant is the One in charge of your well-being and your victory. Confess often that nothing can get to you without first passing through His hands.

Consider this truth. In the beginning, the eating of the fruit caused Adam and Eve to lose victory and authority. Consequently, it was their act of eating that brought us defeat because they ate wrongly. Today, through communion with Christ's blood and body, as we eat in remembrance of Him and what He accomplished on the cross, we proclaim the regaining of the victory and the authority that was originally lost.

In addition to communion, I want you to do something else. I want you to praise God. Not for the bad day, circumstance, or problem you may have. But praise Him because it is not the last word. Praise Him because He is seated high above all rule and authority. And by virtue of your relationship with Him, you are seated with Him. As a result, you have access to His rule and authority in your life. (Ephesians 2:6) This is why we read in the book of Revelation that the believers were able to overcome Satan. In chapter twelve, it is written,

> Now the salvation, and the power, and the kingdom of our God and the authority of His Christ have come, for the accuser of our brethren has been thrown down, he who accuses them before our God day and night. And they overcame him *because of the blood of the Lamb.* . . . (Revelation 12:10–11, emphasis mine)

When the passage states that they overcame him "because of the blood of the Lamb," it is referencing the cross. The believers overcame Satan because they never lost sight that the very thing which was set out to bring hell into their lives did not have the last word. They never lost sight that Jesus' cross conquered Satan, granting them access to an authority higher than Satan's own.

What God wants you to know through these passages in Ephesians, Colossians, and Revelation is that the cross of Jesus Christ has provided victory for you over your enemies. Because Jesus Christ is seated above all rule and authority, you too are seated there with Him. In fact, Paul states exactly that as he continues his letter to the church at Ephesus.

He writes in chapter two, ". . . even when we were dead in our transgressions, *[God the Father]* made us alive together with Christ (by grace you have been saved), and raised us up with Him, and seated us with Him in the heavenly places in Christ Jesus, so that in the ages to come He might show the surpassing riches of His grace in kindness toward us in Christ Jesus" (Ephesians 2:5–7, emphasis mine).

Friend, not only does Jesus Christ have a chair in heaven to sit down in, you have a chair there as well. You have been "seated with Him" above all rule and authority. You have been spiritually relocated. You might be saying, "If I'm seated up there with Jesus, Tony, then why am I not experiencing the victory?"

The answer is simple. It is the same reason why I did not experience the benefits and privileges afforded to me as an American Airlines platinum flyer until I learned what those benefits were and accessed them. If you don't know where you are seated and what exactly that means then you won't access the authority that is yours for the asking.

Physically, you are on earth. Yet, spiritually—you are in heavenly places. However, unless you realize that and operate out of a renewed mindset, you will be confined to what earth has to offer. You must approach your life spiritually in order to attain spiritual authority.

In other words, if all you see is what you see—then

you will never see all there is to be seen. If your eyes are focused on the "here and now," you will miss experiencing heaven's rule in history. Earth's seat doesn't give you authority. Only heaven has access to supreme authority because of what Jesus accomplished on the cross.

When you learn how to function in connection with divine authority, it changes everything. It changes the intimidation factor that others may have over you. It changes your fear levels, worry, dread, and all else that concerns you.

Let me share from my own experience. When I know deep in my spirit that God has shown me something that He is going to do or arrange, the fact that other people say it isn't going to happen or it can't happen doesn't bother me. What other people have to say becomes irrelevant when you function according to the authority of the cross.

When you live in light of Christ's authority, gained for you at the cross, it will change how you walk, talk, and think. It will change your whole approach to life because you realize the difference between power and authority. You realize that what appears to have control in your life doesn't have ultimate control. What appears to have a say in your finances, emotions, health, home, or elsewhere doesn't have the last say.

Friend, before you give up—look up. Fix your eyes on Jesus and see yourself seated with Him in heavenly places. Rejoice because you have been granted full access to His rule and authority, according to the power of God that works in you.

3

THE STABILITY
OF THE CROSS

M y son, Anthony Jr., recently had the opportunity to perform as a guest on NBC's hit program *The Voice*. Through that experience, he was able to publicly testify about Jesus Christ, as well as be a witness to those around him. For the audition round, the contestants on *The Voice* did not get to choose their own song to sing. The song that was chosen for Anthony was "What's Going On" by Marvin Gaye.

Many years ago, Marvin Gaye penned the lyrics of this song, summarizing a number of the negative realities of the world. By asking the question, "What's going on?" he drew attention to the fact that something was amiss and bringing havoc on many dimensions within our world and society.

Members of the church where I serve often pose a similar question to me. They approach me, each with their own burden to bear, and say, "Pastor, what's going on? What is happening?" As we look at the landscape of the society in which we live, a day doesn't go by where more calamity, more chaos, more confusion, and even more uncertainty is not evident.

This uncertainty doesn't just occur in our society in general. There are countless numbers of people who are looking at their own personal lives and struggles and raising the questions, "What is going on with me? What is happening in my life?"

In the twelfth chapter of Hebrews, the author addressed Jewish Christians who were raising the very same question. They were about to enter into the most climactic time that their generation had ever experienced as Jerusalem was about to be besieged by persecution. The temple would soon be destroyed and the dark clouds of despair had already gathered on the horizon. Later on in the book of Hebrews, we even learn that some were imprisoned while the property of others was confiscated.

As you might imagine, in the midst of the pain, turmoil, disruption, and uncertainty, the question emerged: How is a person to respond to the chaos ensuing all around? Thus is the setting for the book of Hebrews.

Prior to chapter twelve, though, the author of Hebrews spent the whole time talking about the Excellency of Jesus Christ. He clearly exalted Jesus over the religious systems of the day, particularly Judaism. In fact, many people were considering going back to Judaism at that time because the Christian worldview and philosophy did not seem to be working for them.

This is the audience that the author was writing to: Christians who are questioning their faith, questioning their beliefs, wanting to know where was the power, stability, and authority that they wanted to experience. To be honest, the culture of this historic audience differs little from those living in our world today.

The foundation of a society we have come to rely on is being shaken to its core. Terrorism reared its ugly head over a decade ago, changing the way we live and view the world and ourselves. During the demise of the financial markets, most of us were robbed to some degree, and many of us to a devastating degree. People who lost their retirement savings and the security of their futures only hope at this point to recover. The opportunity to find a decent paying job has greatly diminished. The American dream, as we once knew it, has eluded many more ever since this downward spiral began.

Not only that, but many families are in disarray. Same-sex marriages are being legalized and even endorsed by the highest office in our land. Divorce continues to shatter both people's present-day lives and the futures of all who have been affected by it. In addition, psychological trauma is at an all-time high. Along with all sorts of addictions, antidepressants, mood-stabilizing drugs, and antianxiety pills have sky-rocketed in usage. More and more people find it difficult to cope with the realities of life as they know it. So much has happened in the last few years to place our nation on the precipice of uncertainty.

In short, we have been shaken. Things that used to look solid and concrete are now made of stucco. Things that used to offer longevity now offer only a temporary assurance. Things that we used to be able to bank on can barely be counted on in any shape or form.

It is in the midst of an environment filled with dire circumstances that the author of Hebrews has given us a word about life after the cross. In it, he makes a distinct contrast between Mt. Sinai and Mt. Zion. On Mt. Sinai, God spoke to Israel in the Old Testament. Then on Mt. Zion, we are introduced to the new covenant given to us by the blood of Jesus Christ shed on the cross. It is under the tenets and truths of Mt. Zion that we find ourselves today. It is precisely because of the cross of Jesus Christ that we no longer live under the terror of Mt. Sinai.

The writer of Hebrews described what life under Mt. Sinai was like when he wrote,

> For you have not come to a mountain that can be touched and to a blazing fire, and to darkness and gloom and whirlwind, and to the blast of a trumpet and the sound of words which sound was such that those who heard begged that no further word be spoken to them. For they could not bear the command, "If even a beast touches the mountain, it will be stoned." And so terrible was the sight, that Moses

said, "I am full of fear and trembling." (Hebrews 12:18–21)

For us to fully actualize, realize, and maximize the power and stability of the cross, we need to recall what life was like before it. When God came down and spoke prior to giving the Ten Commandments, it was a sight to behold as the mountain began to smoke and quake. These environmental aspects happened in order to let the people know how serious a moment that it was. God's presence on the mountain shook the entire mountain so much so that the people ran away; they did not want to listen. Even Moses himself trembled.

Friend, the holiness and the perfection of God are so great that to even be near Him shakes things up. Yet, on the cross Jesus Christ has given us access to the God of the universe. On the cross, Jesus Christ offered Himself as the Mediator between God and man. It was there that He initiated the new covenant.

Because you are a believer, you must understand this: Mt. Sinai is not your mountain. Mt Zion is your mountain. As the writer continues, we learn about this access and mediation that is available to us. We read,

But you have come to Mount Zion and to the city of the living God, the heavenly Jerusalem, and to myriads of angels, to the general assembly and church of the firstborn who are enrolled in heaven, and to God, the Judge of all, and to the spirits of the righteous

made perfect, and to Jesus, the mediator of a new
covenant, and to the sprinkled blood, which speaks
better than the blood of Abel. (Hebrews 12:22–24)

In this passage, you find that you have been moved to
a new city. You are operating in a new environment while
living in a new realm. You are not living at Mt. Sinai
where there is terror, trembling, and insecurity. Because of
what Jesus accomplished at the cross, that is not your
home as a believer in Jesus Christ.

Why is this so? The blood of Jesus Christ has or-
chestrated a new covenant. Therefore, you are functioning underneath the umbrella of a whole new realm. You
have access to a whole new way of life because Jesus has
served as Mediator between you and God. Through
Christ's atoning blood, God has set up a brand new
arrangement whereby He is committed to you by a new
covenant.

Keep in mind, this new covenant is based on blood
"which speaks better than the blood of Abel." Abel's blood
was shed by Cain, and Scripture tells us that it spoke from
the ground. We read where God addressed Cain, "The
voice of your brother's blood is crying to Me from the
ground" (Genesis 4:10). Abel's blood called out from the
ground, crying for justice. When God heard the cry for
justice, He responded to Cain. This is because the blood
spoke judgment.

But the writer of Hebrews wants you to know that
"justice blood" is not the blood he is talking about. He

explains that the blood, which was shed at the cross, mediated an entirely different arrangement with God. It cried out for an entirely different response from God. Christ's blood called for the new covenant, mercy, and commitment.

Therefore, when things in your life seem messed up, shaken, and uncertain, you need to view God and His relationship with you through the lens of this new arrangement that the cross represents. Otherwise, you will get it all wrong.

> # GOD HAS SOMETHING THAT HE WANTS TO NOT ONLY TELL YOU BUT ALSO TO DEVELOP IN YOU.

Through the next section in Hebrews, we receive insight into how we are to view God when our lives begin to unravel and become unstable. We read,

See to it that you do not refuse Him who is speaking. For if those did not escape when they refused him who warned them on earth, much less will we escape who turn away from Him who warns from heaven. And His voice *shook* the earth then, but now He has promised, saying, "Yet once more I will *shake* not only the earth, but also the heaven." This expression, "Yet once more," denotes the removing of those things which can be *shaken*, as of created things, so that those things which cannot be *shaken* may remain. (Hebrews 12:25–27, emphasis mine)

If you are struggling today, please note that in this passage the author repeatedly used the word "shaken" or a derivative thereof. If your world has been shaken—your personal life, emotions, finances, career, or anything else has been shook up—you are not alone. If it has become difficult for you to sleep peacefully at night, then you know your life has been shaken. If it has become harder for you to focus like you used to, you know that your world has become shaken. If it has become a challenge for you to find happiness in the things that used to make you happy, your world has been shaken. During times like these you may feel afraid, angry, unstable, and insecure.

Nevertheless, when any of that happens, as a believer in Jesus Christ, I want you to remember that you are a part of the new covenant. You belong to a group of people uniquely attached to the cross of Christ and all that it entails. As a result, God has a different end goal for the "shaking" you experience in life. Because of the cross, you are now enabled to hear Him.

God's goal is not simply to announce His presence and then lead you to fear, awe, and trembling to such a degree that you beg Him to leave because you cannot bear it. No, rather His objective is to announce His presence in order to draw you close to Him. God has something that He wants to not only tell you but also to develop in you. Remember we read, "See to it that you do not refuse Him who is speaking" (Hebrews 12:25).

You must understand that God is talking to us and He has something very important to say.

When I was a young child and an enormous thunderstorm would gather in the heavens, my grandmother would always make me turn off the television or the radio because, as she put it, "God is talking." So we would all sit there in the silence of the moment, as "God talked." Actually, it was just thunder, but the idea holds true when things become shaky in your life. Know that through the clatter of your circumstances, God is talking and He wants you to listen.

You know how it is on days when bad weather occurs or even the anticipation of inclement weather? At those times we frequently tune into, or pull up on our computers, the weather report. Typically, we give the reporter our undivided focus and attention. Especially if you hear that there is a hurricane or a tornado in the vicinity, the only voice you are listening to is the person giving the weather report. You tune in because things are starting to get shaky. And when things get shaky, they need to be treated accordingly.

Friend, when God allows, or even causes, things to be shaken nationally, locally, or even personally, know this: do not "refuse Him who is speaking." God is talking. In fact, the shakier things get, the louder He is speaking.

I have four children and, at the time of this writing, ten grandchildren. Having experienced, to varying degrees, the births of fourteen babies over the years, I can say without any hesitation that the act of labor and subsequent delivery of a child is an intense, painful, shaky experience. Anguish manifests itself because the baby is speaking. Now, obviously the baby is not speaking in words that can be heard or understood, but the baby is definitely sending a message. The message being quite simply, "I want out!" When the baby in the womb starts to speak that message, everyone listens.

The delivery of a newborn child is a powerful message of separation. What is about to occur is a separation from the mother and the baby. The life of a human is being removed from within the mother and that removal process hurts. The pain indicates that it is time for a change. In fact, as the pain intensifies, the closer to the separation and change the mother is.

Keep this in mind. The separation is good news coming through a bad situation. It is a bad situation because it is painful. Any mother will tell you it hurts. We can't deny that it hurts. But the good news is that there is new life about to be made known and it is time for the manifestation.

Whenever God was ready to do something special, unique, and wonderful throughout Scripture, it would be introduced through a painful scenario. God either allowed, or created, anguish and pain in order to introduce the new situation. Frequently, when God is ready to do something new in our lives, He knows that we are not ready for it. We are too set in our ways, tied to our past, and attached to a wrong way of thinking to accept change.

Consequently, there are a multitude of things that God must do to evoke a change within us before the new thing can happen. In other words, because we are not ready, He makes us ready. A separation from what we previously depended upon must occur so that we will not only look to Him but also be able to see Him.

For example, when the Israelites crossed the Red Sea, they only crossed the Red Sea because God blocked them in and there was no way out. They had Pharaoh on one side and the Red Sea on the other, and so they found themselves in an uncertain situation. All they could see in whatever direction they looked was death.

The Israelites would have never seen God do the miraculous if they had not been positioned to such a degree that they needed the miraculous. God had to force the issue with the Israelites by creating and allowing such turbulence in their lives so that He could birth the next thing that He wanted to reveal to them about Himself.

In shaking things up, or in allowing painful scenarios to occur in our lives, God is essentially eroding one realm in order to expose us to another realm. He is eroding earth in order to manifest heaven. The reason why He must erode the old world order from us is because we are too attached—too dependent—on it. As a result, He must shake us loose from the things, beliefs, or even people that we depend on too heavily before He can take us to the place He wants us to be.

God does this by creating discontinuity, disconnection, and destabilization in our lives. This, in turn, is designed to remove us from our loyalty to earth, and the ways of earth, so that we can witness the movement of heaven and the new covenant brought to us through the cross.

When God either allows or creates discontinuity in your life, He is speaking. He is saying something particularly with regard to your relationship to His new covenant with you. What He is saying is that He wants to disconnect you from the things, thoughts, or people of this world order so that He can reveal to you eternal things. As long as you are too attached, or too dependent, on anything other than God and His relationship with you, you are not hearing Him. Consequently, that means He must continue to turn up the heat in your life.

See, you only feel the heat because your attachment to that which He is trying to reveal to you is of temporal value rather than eternal value. Consider this. When you are in an earthquake, you are going to feel and experience the shaking and trembling of the earth. However, if you are in an airplane flying over an earthquake, you won't feel its effects. This is because you are no longer attached to that which is shaking.

By means of the cross, God wants to flow into and through you the blessings of the new covenant, but in order to do so He must disconnect you from anything that is inconsistent with this covenant and the relationship that He desires to have with you.

Essentially, He wants to remove the things in your life that do not add to His relationship with you and His purpose for you. He removes that which can be removed, that which in and of itself is not where your foundation should be. In this way, your foundation—your relationship with Him through the cross of Christ—will remain.

Let's hear this again from Scripture, "'Yet once more,' denotes the removing of those things which can be shaken, as of created things, so that those things which cannot be shaken may remain" (Hebrews 12:27). The phrase "Yet once more" is a reference from the book of Haggai where the prophet Haggai spoke of God's statement that He would shake the nations in order to restore His glory in His temple. We read,

> For thus says the Lord of hosts, "*Once more* in a little while, I am going to shake the heavens and the earth, the sea also and the dry land. I will shake all the nations; and they will come with the wealth of all nations, and I will fill this house with glory," says the Lord of hosts. (Haggai 2:6–7, emphasis mine)

The writer of Hebrews quotes the prophet Haggai where God said that He is going to shake things up in order to transfer things over. An easy way to get a picture of this is by comparing it to a child's piggy bank. The child's piggy bank would need to be shaken and shaken in order to get out the valuable items from within it. God says He is going to "shake" things up in order to shake something loose from one realm and deliver it to another, His own.

> # YOU SEE, IF SOMETHING CAN BE SHAKEN IN YOUR LIFE, IT IS NOT OF HIM.

What the blood of Christ did on the cross was mediate a new arrangement—a new realm—that God has with every believer, as well as with His church. That new arrangement is called the new covenant. Yet, in order for this new covenant to manifest itself in your life, God needs to first disconnect you from the illegitimate blockages in the arteries of your spirit. He needs to remove your attachment and dependency on that which is not Him. God has to remove that attachment because it is standing in the way of your relationship to Him.

Some of the greatest memories in my life have come out of a crisis where heaven had to step in because earth couldn't fix it. That is to say, a problem I was experiencing. By "earth," I mean earth's program, thoughts, and processes. During those times, I realized firsthand that whatever it was that I had previously depended upon, even if it was myself, it could be shaken. Yet, there was one thing that remained constant throughout and was able to eventually come in and resolve the situation. Even if the problem was not solved right away, there was always one stabilizing factor for me within the situation—God.

This is because in the book of Hebrews we read that God shakes things in order to remove that which can be shaken. You see, if something can be shaken in your life, it is not of Him. God deserves all the praise because what He offers, through the cross, is unshakeable. It is dependable, strong, and stable. We read,

> Therefore, since we receive *a kingdom which cannot be shaken*, let us show gratitude, by which we may offer to God an acceptable service with reverence and awe; for our God is a consuming fire. (Hebrews 12:28–29, emphasis mine)

What the cross of Jesus Christ has done is given each of us the transference from that which can be shaken into an unshakeable kingdom. You have received entrance into a kingdom that cannot be shaken. It is not subject to any events happening around you. Friend, if you are only looking at the stock-market pages, the banking system, your job, co-workers, family members, health, relationships, or anything else you can see—you are looking at things that can be affected by what goes on around them. If that is all you can see, you will be shaken.

Instead, if you fix your eyes on the stability of the cross of Jesus Christ, you cannot be destabilized. This is because you are operating with the rule of a different King and under a different authority than the world. At times when you feel like your world is falling apart, make sure you don't refuse to listen to God. He is speaking to you. He is trying to pry you loose from what He knows cannot offer you long-term peace, strength, wisdom, or stability.

When your world is crumbling all around you, if you will keep your eyes on Jesus Christ and the promise of the new covenant that He has given you through the cross, you will not crumble along with it.

One of my favorite stories in the Bible takes place on the wall of Jericho. It is a principle that we often fail to take into account. So many times, preachers or teachers will wax eloquently on Joshua and his army marching around Jericho until the walls fell down. Yet a detail that is often left out is what happened to one portion of the wall. Despite any images you may have seen drawn in children's Bible storybooks or some other biblical artwork on the subject, the entire wall of Jericho did not fall down.

While everything crumbled and shook in and around Jericho that day, the house where a woman named Rahab lived remained intact. Rahab's home was located in the outer portion of the Jericho wall (Joshua 2:15). When she welcomed the spies into her home and hid them from her own government in order to protect them, she aligned herself with the Israelites and their covenantal relationship with God.

As a result, when the kingdom of which she was physically and geographically associated, Jericho, fell apart—her home and her family within it were safe. This is because Rahab chose to align herself with another King, the only One from an unshakeable kingdom. She had placed herself under the covering and covenant of God.

It is truly significant to highlight that the Jericho wall did fall, except for one piece of it where a prostitute named Rahab placed a scarlet rope outside her window. In doing so, she demonstrated her subjection to and alignment with the one true God.

On the cross, Jesus' life became our scarlet rope as it aligned each of us who place our faith in Him underneath the covering of the new covenant. While things around you may become shaky, when you fix your eyes on Jesus, you will remember the promise of His covenant and that you belong to an unshakeable kingdom.

There will be trials in this life. God frequently uses these trials to reveal to you that which can be shaken so that it will also be removed from you. He is a jealous God. Moreover, as we saw earlier, "our God is a consuming fire." What that means penned within the biblical context is a reference to the consuming fire that consumed the sacrifice placed on the altar in the temple and burned it up.

In the Old Testament times, the purpose of the sacrifice was to render judgment in order to free God up to continue giving the blessings. This act of judgment served as purification between God and man. What Christ did on the cross was act on our behalf in light of God as a "consuming fire." His death allows us to experience God in such a way that we must show Him our sincere gratitude—for He is our foundation and the stability of our lives.

Therefore, when things heat up in your life, know that God is not bringing judgment on you. He is not trying to chase you away. Yes, He may be disciplining you because God disciplines those whom He loves. He may also be trying to separate you from that which you should not be so entirely attached to or dependent on. But know that He is not judging you to punish you. Christ took our punishment on the cross. God has a goal in mind for the trials and pain that enter our lives. That goal is to shift us into a daily experience of His unshakeable kingdom.

Consider this analogy. When you wake up in the morning and you need to wear a nice outfit to work or to church, you will often want to iron your clothes before putting them on. This is because you don't want wrinkled clothing to reflect you poorly to those around you. So what you do is take out your iron, plug it in, and let it get too hot to the touch. Then you slowly move it back and forth over the wrinkles in your clothes.

Your clothes feel the heat, the pressure, and the sting of the iron. You aren't putting the hot iron on your clothes because you want to burn them. You are not trying to destroy them. You are simply trying to improve them and return them to their intended look. In this case, your iron becomes a consuming fire. It doesn't consume the clothes; it consumes the wrinkles in the clothes. It separates the bends and the folds from the material.

The reason why you take so much time to iron out your clothes by applying both heat and pressure to them is because you plan on wearing your clothes. You know that if you wear them with the wrinkles, it is going to make you look bad. Since you don't want to look bad, you place the heat of the consuming fire on them.

Because our God is a consuming fire, He renders discipline on the things which do not belong in our lives. He removes the things which can be shaken so that we can fully experience the unshakeable stability of Him. The reason why He will allow heat in your life is to separate you from the elements of your life which do not bring Him glory. Why? It is because He has chosen to wear you as a reflection of Himself to others. He wants you to glorify Him through your life. He longs to bless you, but He wants to make sure you are capable of receiving that blessing in faith.

The cross has given you a new arrangement with God, placing you in a kingdom that does not shake in spite of the shaking all around you. Therefore, in the midst of what troubles you, as bad as it may seem—or as strong as the labor pains may feel—trust Him. Listen to Him. Look to Him. Honor Him. Respond to Him. Have faith in Him. He is not trying to hurt you. He is simply trying to reveal to you the things in your life that are of no eternal value. Many times they are of little temporal value as well.

The cross is your comfort. It is your reminder that what you are experiencing is not judgment. In fact, it is just the opposite. Always remember, the trials in your life are there to reveal the treasure of the new covenant and the stability and permanence that comes with alignment under God. They are designed to release you from, or to have you release, that which can be shaken in order to grow and expand your experience with that which cannot: God and His unshakeable kingdom.

4

THE IDENTIFICATION
WITH THE CROSS

On one occasion, a man went to a psychiatrist because he was having some problems. They were serious problems so he thought he needed to seek out a serious solution. Entering the psychiatrist's cozy and neatly decorated office, the man took a seat. Then he headed straight into his problem.

"Doc," he said. The doctor kept his eyes directly on him and nodded his head, urging him gently to continue.

"Doc, something's wrong," the man blurted out.

"What's the problem, sir?" the doctor asked, trying to get more information.

"Well, every time I go to the supermarket, I am drawn to the dog food aisle. I just want to be around the dog food. In fact, I love to eat dog food."

The doctor shifted his weight in his chair and decided to search for some background on this man's issue. "How long have you been struggling with this problem?" the doctor asked patiently.

"Ever since I was a puppy," the man replied.

You see, how you perceive yourself will determine what you seek after. If you perceive yourself as a puppy then you will naturally want to find some dog food. In other words, your identity is critical to your behavior, habits, and ways of operating.

Many Christians today are confused about who they are. In turn, this brings about confusion in how they are to function. We operate in the manner that we do because of how we perceive ourselves to be. Subsequently, if your self-perception is incorrect, your function will be errant as well.

Furthermore, we often want to change what we do without first having a clear understanding of who we are. This is actually operating in reverse. When a Christian says, "I am an addict," then we should not be surprised that he or she acts that addiction out because that is who we were told that they were. Your self-identification influences your practice. If this same Christian says, "I am a blood-bought child of the King who can do all things through Christ who strengthens me," we should be surprised if that person continues to give in to addiction. What you think influences what you do.

In fact, a friend of mine works at a drug rehab center. One of the best in the nation, the facility uses nothing more than Scripture to help its patients overcome their addictions. This is because when you meditate on and memorize the truth of who you are and the power of the One who loves you, you have all you need to live a victorious life. The mind is a powerful thing. It is the root of all defeats as well as all successes.

Therefore, if you are going to live out your destiny and achieve the greatness that God has in store for you, rather than settle for just getting by, you must first change what you think. In particular, you must change what you think about the cross of Christ. The cross of Jesus Christ does not merely symbolize an event that happened two thousand years ago on Calvary.

The cross of Jesus Christ is just as relevant today as it was in that day. It is not simply an icon around which we celebrate Easter each year. Rather, it is the very definition of your success as a believer. It is to be the centerpiece of your personal reference and your identity.

The summing up of who you are as a Christian and who God has designed you to be is found in my life verse, Galatians 2:20. Truly, before my feet hit the floor each morning, I say this verse as a reminder of who I am and how I am to approach my day.

Before we look at this verse in detail, though, I want to set up the context for it. Beginning in verse eleven of the second chapter of Galatians, we discover the disciple Peter eating ham sandwiches, chitlins, and pigs' feet with the Gentiles. Peter was enjoying a good meal with a group of people who did not typically associate with the

Jews. In turn, the Jews did not typically associate with them. While eating, some of his Jewish brothers show up. Not wanting to offend his own race, Peter withdraws from his association with the Gentiles. In essence, he caved in to peer pressure.

> # THE TRUTH IS, ALL SOCIAL, ECONOMIC, FAMILIAL, POLITICAL, PERSONAL, AND OTHER ISSUES CAN BE TRACED BACK TO A SPIRITUAL AND THEOLOGICAL ROOT.

Seeing what he did, Paul confronts Peter. We read that Peter "stood condemned" (Galatians 2:11). It wasn't that Peter wasn't a Christian or that he wasn't saved, the issue was that Peter was not functioning in light of his identification with his faith. Rather, he was functioning in light of his identification with his culture.

We know this because Paul went on to write, "But when I saw that they were not straightforward about the truth of the gospel . . ." (Galatians 2:14). In other words, when Paul saw that Peter and his friends' social decision (who they were going to eat with) wasn't being defined by their gospel belief system, they were then warping the message and testimony of what the gospel means in everyday life.

Here was a spiritual, theological issue that brought rise to a social problem. The truth is, all social, economic, familial, political, personal, and other issues can be traced back to a spiritual and theological root. One of our problems today is our unwillingness, or possibly our ignorance, in making a tie between the social and the spiritual. The result is syncretism with the culture rather than identification with the cross, thus removing the power that comes through our alignment with Jesus Christ.

If you received Jesus Christ as your Savior, a crucifixion has occurred. In fact, two crucifixions have occurred: Jesus on the cross and you. Paul tells us in Galatians 2:20 what the secret to living a life of power and purpose really is when he writes,

> I have been crucified with Christ; and it is no longer I who live, but Christ lives in me; and the life which I now live in the flesh I live by faith in the Son of God, who loved me and gave Himself up for me. (Galatians 2:20)

On the cross, there was a dual death that occurred. In the spiritual realm, what happened in history some two thousand years ago happened in you the moment you trusted Jesus Christ for your salvation. A union occurred that is not only theological but also practical. In fact, it may be the most important practical application of Scripture that you could ever know. The key to all things related to life, victory, and power lies in this one truth revealed in Galatians 2:20.

When you accepted Jesus Christ as your Savior, a legal transaction occurred. You were justified because of His blood and made one with Him. This is similar to a marriage when two people are united and become "one flesh," as demonstrated in physical intimacy. The problems in marriage typically arise when one or both parties try to live other than as "one flesh."

The problems in your Christian life result from the same issue. However, since Jesus Christ is the perfect, sinless Deity, problems occur solely when you try to live apart from Him. Once you've "jumped the broom" and stepped into the family of God, you are a new creation, made one with Christ. Granted, you have dragged a lot of your unsaved thinking, actions, fears, anxieties, and desires into the new relationship.

Just like a daughter who marries young, you are inclined to falling back on the history of what you've known and experienced before your union with Christ. A daughter who spent twenty-some years under the influence and care of her father may struggle to transfer that allegiance and identity to her young husband. This, as you may know or have seen, causes great conflict in a marriage.

Likewise, a similar mentality of bringing your way of thinking, acting, and believing into your relationship with Jesus Christ sets up a series of conflicts as well. To be crucified with Jesus Christ establishes a brand new reference point for how you view yourself, other people, your circumstances, and life in general. However, what many believers will do in their Christian lives is become one with Jesus Christ at salvation and then attempt to disconnect Him from their thinking, actions, choices, decisions, and all else in their lives.

For example, when I drink coffee in the morning, I will always pour some cream or some milk into my coffee. After I stir it, my coffee and the cream are now one. There is no way that I could possibly disconnect the coffee from the cream once I've stirred it. In the same way, the union between Christ and a believer is still there. But instead of embracing his or her new identity and relationship with Christ, some individuals wind up with a big mess and a lot of wasted time and effort.

Paul gives us the secret to the success of maximizing our union with the cross in the book of 1 Corinthians when he asserted, "I die daily" (1 Corinthians 15:31). To be crucified means to die. According to Paul, that death ought to occur daily. To die simply means to place our wants, thoughts, motives, and desires on the altar of Jesus Christ and pick up His wants, thoughts, motives, and desires instead.

It is a dying to self that gives you the ability to truly live. Jesus' life in you only comes when you willingly lay down your own life and submit to Him. In other words, you choose His will over your own. It is a conscious decision that says God's way supersedes your way. God's choice supersedes your choice. By this voluntary surrender, you will experience the fullness of the abundant life that has been promised to you through the death and resurrection of Jesus Christ.

> ## AS LONG AS YOU ARE LIVING FOR YOU, ALL THAT THE CROSS HAS TO OFFER WILL NEVER BE YOURS.

So many of us fail to carry this out and then wonder why we are not experiencing all of God's promises. We die to Him in salvation but then we live for ourselves in our daily choices. We wonder why we fail to have the victory that is ours and live instead in perpetual defeat. The truth is, there can be no resurrection without a crucifixion. You don't get the miracle without surrendering to God in the first place.

For example, you probably own several home appliances, with each one having a unique responsibility. The refrigerator keeps things cold. The stove makes things hot. The toaster toasts things. Can openers open things, and so on. But there is one thing that each appliance holds in common—none of them function for themselves. The refrigerator does not keep the food cold so that it can eat the food. The stove does not heat the food so that it can eat the food either. The toaster doesn't toast bread and the can opener doesn't open something in order to consume the food.

Each appliance that you purchased exists to serve you. If it didn't, my guess is that you would no longer keep it in your home. This is the reason why appliances are bought and paid for—so the one who bought and paid for them would benefit from them. The purpose for the purchase was that the thing purchased might benefit the purchaser.

Friend, you were bought with a price—the shed blood of Jesus Christ. You exist for the Purchaser, not for yourself. The moment you flip that and begin making your decisions in light of your own thoughts, you have lost your identity. You have lost the reason for your being here. You will never experience all that the Christian life was meant to be, and you will never actualize all of the power you are supposed to have. That is, unless and until you realize that you do not exist for you.

As long as you are living for you, all that the cross has to offer will never be yours. It will remain as an historical event that happened some two thousand years ago rather than as a daily experience ushering you into the greatest moments and meaning of your life.

If you could ask Paul what his plans were for the day, he would reply, "I don't have plans because dead people don't plan." But what if Paul were still alive and you changed the question a little bit. You could ask, "Paul, what are God's plans for you?" He would say, "Okay, let's talk."

Paul could have a conversation all day long because he aligned his thinking with God's thinking. He made God's will, his will. He made seeking God's face and God's perspective as the single most important thing in his life. Because of how he functioned, Paul experienced things on earth that those around him did not experience. He saw many miracles and demonstrations of power. On numerous occasions, he was given the personal ability to overcome adversities. In fact, he was even taken up to the "third heaven" and ushered into an intimate experience unlike any other.

Paul got it. He understood what it meant to identify with the cross of Christ. And because he did, he received all that was his to receive in Christ Jesus.

A key to understanding how to identify with the cross comes when Paul described his own identity in Galatians 2:20, "the life which I now live in the flesh *I live by faith in the Son of God*, who loved me and gave Himself up for me" (emphasis mine). Some versions have translated this phrase to read, "I live by faith *of* the Son of God."

The word "of" is a more accurate translation from the original text and gives a clearer definition of how we are to live our lives victoriously. What Paul means when he wrote that he lived by faith "of" the Son of God is that he lived his days Monday through Sunday not so much by his own faith in Jesus, but by his faith in Jesus' faith in Jesus.

I know that may sound a little tricky but the truth it contains is profound. It is not just that we are to believe in Jesus Christ, but we are to believe in Jesus' belief in Himself. It is because of your full confidence that Jesus has full confidence in Himself that you discover the ability to piggyback on Him.

> # DON'T WORRY ABOUT HOW MUCH FAITH YOU HAVE, WORRY ABOUT WHAT YOU PLACE IT IN.

Have you ever taken a child on a piggyback ride? Do you know what that child believes in? That child does not just believe in you, he or she believes that you believe in you. Children rely on the fact that you have confidence in your ability. That is why they will ask, "Do you have me?" In other words, they are asking, "Do you believe that you have me?" This is because even though they may have doubts, if you believe then they will believe in your belief.

In a similar way, it's not simply your faith in Jesus that gives you the ability to experience the abundant life. It is your faith in Jesus' faith in Himself that opens the door. You don't have to worry about how much faith you have—even weak faith can accomplish much if it is placed on that which is worthy of it. Jesus said that faith as small as a mustard seed can move a mountain.

Therefore, it's not the size of your faith that matters; it is the object of your faith that matters. That is the key. If you have a lot of faith in a little thing, you don't have enough to do anything. But if you have a little faith in a big thing, then you have more than enough to do everything.

Even if your faith in Jesus is small, it will still work wonders because Jesus' faith in Jesus is huge. Don't worry about how much faith you have, worry about what you place it in. Piggyback on Jesus because He's got you.

Consider this example. A high jumper typically tries to clear seven feet. He backs up, gets in his stance, takes off running, lifts his foot up, and then jumps over with all of the effort that he can muster. He tries to get as high as he can go. The high jumper believes he can do it and he does as much as he can. If he knocks over the pole, he goes back and tries harder the next time.

On the other hand, when a pole vaulter tries to clear a pole, he will typically try to get over a much higher level, even more than double of what the high jumper will attempt. This is because the pole vaulter has a pole in his hands and he's not merely resting on his own ability to make it. He is resting in his confidence in the pole, trusting that the pole has enough strength and elasticity to do what is needed to be done in order to propel him to victory. The pole vaulter is banking on what he is attached to rather than simply on himself. Because of this, he is able to go higher and farther than he ever could on his own.

Too many Christians today are trying to get by on their own. Maybe you are one of them. You run as fast as you can, jump as high as you can, and work as hard as you can. Still, you don't go nearly as far as you can were you to rely on your attachment to the cross of Jesus Christ. If you will link yourself up with the pole of His cross, He has the ability and the willingness to propel you higher than you ever thought you could soar. But that takes faith. It takes dependence. It takes identifying with Jesus daily over merely identifying with yourself, the world, your friends, or anything else that you place before Him.

When you put Jesus first and rely on Him, you will not regret it. It is because of Paul's intimate and daily identification with Jesus Christ and the meaning behind His cross that Paul was able to write in his letter to the church at Philippi, "I can do all things through Him who strengthens me" (Philippians 4:13).

For most Christians, this verse is just a cute saying. It is a nice sounding spiritual platitude to quote. I have met precious few believers who take it literally and comprehend how to live the full life of identification with Jesus Christ. These are the believers who will experience the fullness of His power.

Paul was in that category. For him, the words he penned weren't just a cute thing to say. Paul knew that he was attached to a pole that could hurl him higher than he could ever get on his own. In fact, it hurled him so high that he wound up in the third heaven. Friend, that's very high. This happened not because Paul had a whole bunch of faith but rather because Paul believed that Jesus had faith in Himself.

The apostle Paul taught us that it is Christ in him, and Christ in you, that produces the faith for victory. In his letter to the church at Colossae, he writes, "to whom God willed to make known what is the riches of the glory of this mystery among the Gentiles, which is Christ in you, the hope of glory" (Colossians 1:27).

Paul's goal for the believers he was ministering to and encouraging was that Christ would be manifest in their mortal bodies. He knew that when Jesus Christ is made manifest in a believer's life, the believer begins to function supernaturally rather than naturally. Believers have access to the abundant life promised in Scripture through abiding with Christ.

I cannot emphasize this enough. What keeps Jesus Christ from being made manifest in your life is when you live for yourself rather than for Him. It is when you do not die daily—you do not take up your cross—you do not become crucified with Him on an ongoing basis. That is the single most, greatest deterrent to experiencing all of the supernatural power and victory God has in store for you. As long as you are living for yourself and the cross remains a distant thought from an even more distant past, you will not fully maximize the life you were made to live.

Friend, you can't identify with the cross of Jesus by following rules. In fact, the cross did away with the system of rules and replaced it with a relationship. You can't achieve this victory or access this power through checking off a list. It has to be done through having a love that both honors and trusts in Jesus' belief in Himself and what He has accomplished.

To say that the cross alone is not enough is to diminish what the cross attained. To add anything to the cross —works, self-righteousness, duty, or whatever else—is to nullify the fullness of His love for you. It is to spit on the cross. I know that is a graphic way to look at what you think you might be doing to live a Christian life. But you must understand that the cross accomplished everything for you already. To add to it is to lessen what Jesus already did.

Paul followed up after his verse on being crucified with Christ with this very thought. He wrote, "I do not nullify the grace of God, for if righteousness comes through the Law, then Christ died needlessly" (Galatians 2:21). To "nullify" something is to cancel it out. When you pursue religion over a relationship with Jesus Christ, you have canceled out the grace of God in your life—the awesome gift that the cross of Christ achieved for you.

God is free to rain down His grace upon you because of what Jesus did on the cross. You have hope simply because Christ is in you: "Christ in you, the hope of glory." In order for God's grace to flow in your life, your focus must be on Him. It must be on Jesus. It must be on the cross. Your identity must daily be in His crucifixion.

The bad news for the majority of Christianity today from what I can tell is that, although many are Christians, few seem to know Jesus. Jesus is not in the vicinity simply because there is no living connection to Him. Yes, there is a legal tie, but there is no love relationship. When you cancel the relationship, you cancel—or nullify—the flow of God's grace to you.

Let me explain this with a concrete example. Let's say your refrigerator is not working. Your ice cream is melting and your food is beginning to spoil. So you go online and research how to fix your refrigerator. You find a manual for your model and it shows you all of the parts for your refrigerator. You spend a lot of time studying this manual. You read the book thoroughly. And, as you do, you attempt to apply what you learned. You twist that and turn this. You move that and adjust this.

Yet, no matter how much you apply from the instructions, nothing seems to be working. In fact, all you have done is frustrated yourself and wasted your time while your food rots even further. There is nothing in your refrigerator that is fresh any more.

You've studied the book. You've examined the book. You really want your refrigerator to work. In fact, you have gotten down on your hands and knees to tighten things up. You have done this for hours, now with perspiration running down your face.

Finally, after all you've done, someone comes up to you and gives you a suggestion. "Why don't you plug it in?"

Friend, no matter how hard you try and no matter how hard you work, you will have only wasted your time and your life if you do not live connected to the power of the cross of Jesus Christ. You can go to church every single day of the week if you want to. You can read the Bible from cover to cover. You can study it, repeat it, and tell others about it. In fact, you can try and do what it says to do all day long. But if you have cancelled out the flow of God's grace in your life due to a nullification of the cross and your relationship with Jesus Christ, it won't mean a thing.

God is not free to flow His power through you if you are not identified with the cross. Until you make the decision that you will die to yourself and live to Him, you will continue to simply exist rather than maximize the destiny God intended for you to have.

A lot of believers today are blocking what God wants to do in them and through them because they are trying to get there in their own strength. Sadly, in doing so, they cut the cord through which grace flows. Doing the best you can and trying harder every day is not what God wants from you. He wants your heart. He wants your surrender to Him. He wants you to trust Him, love Him, and experience Him. He wants a relationship. In that relationship, He wants for you to have all that is yours by virtue of Christ's sacrifice on the cross.

THE URBAN
ALTERNATIVE

D r. Tony Evans and The Urban Alternative (TUA) equips, **empowers**, and **unites** Christians to **impact** *individuals, families, churches,* and *communities* to restore hope and transform lives.

We believe the core cause of the problems we face in our personal lives, homes, churches, and societies is a spiritual one; therefore, the only way to address them is spiritually. We've tried a political, a social, an economic, and even a religious agenda. It's time for a Kingdom Agenda— God's visible and comprehensive rule over every area of life because when we function as we were designed, there is a divine power that changes everything. It renews and restores as the life of Christ is made manifest within our own. As we align ourselves under Him, there is an alignment that happens from deep within—where He brings about full restoration. It is an atmosphere that revives and makes whole.

As it impacts us, it impacts others—transforming every sphere of life in which we live. When each biblical sphere of life functions in accordance with God's Word, the outcomes are evangelism, discipleship, and community impact. As we learn how to govern ourselves under God, we then transform the institutions of family, church, and society from a biblically based kingdom perspective. Through Him, we are touching heaven and changing earth.

To achieve our goal, we use a variety of strategies, methods, and resources for reaching and equipping as many people as possible.

BROADCAST MEDIA

Hundreds of thousands of individuals experience *The Alternative with Dr. Tony Evans* through the daily radio broadcast playing on more than **850 radio outlets** and in more than **80 countries**. The broadcast can also be seen on several television networks and is viewable online at TonyEvans.org.

LEADERSHIP TRAINING

The Kingdom Agenda Pastors (KAP) provides a *viable network* for *like-minded pastors* who embrace the Kingdom

Agenda philosophy. Pastors have the opportunity to go deeper with Dr. Tony Evans as they are given greater biblical knowledge, practical applications, and resources to impact individuals, families, churches, and communities. KAP welcomes senior and associate pastors of all churches.

The Kingdom Agenda Pastors' Summit progressively develops church leaders to meet the demands of the 21st century while maintaining the gospel message and the strategic position of the church. The Summit introduces *intensive seminars, workshops,* and *resources,* addressing issues affecting the community, family, leadership, organizational health, and more.

Pastors' Wives Ministry, founded by Dr. Lois Evans, provides *counsel, encouragement,* and *spiritual resources* for pastors' wives as they serve with their husbands in the ministry. A primary focus of the ministry is the KAP Summit that offers senior pastors' wives a safe place to *reflect, renew,* and *relax* along with training in personal development, spiritual growth, and care for their emotional and physical well-being.

COMMUNITY IMPACT

National Church Adopt-A-School Initiative (NCAASI) prepares churches across the country to impact communities by using *public schools as the primary vehicle for effecting positive social change* in urban youth and families. Leaders of churches, school districts, faith-based organizations, and other nonprofit organizations are equipped with the knowledge and tools to *forge partnerships* and build *strong social service delivery systems.*

This training is based on the comprehensive church-based community impact strategy conducted by Oak Cliff Bible Fellowship. It addresses such areas as economic development, education, housing, health revitalization, family renewal, and racial reconciliation. We also assist churches in tailoring the model to meet the specific needs of their communities while simultaneously addressing the spiritual and moral frame of reference.

RESOURCE DEVELOPMENT

We are fostering lifelong learning partnerships with the people we serve by providing a variety of published materials. We offer booklets, Bible studies, books, CDs, and DVDs to strengthen people in their walk with God and ministry to others.

* * *

For more information, a catalog of Dr. Tony Evans'
ministry resources, and a complimentary copy of
Dr. Evans' devotional newsletter,
call (800) 800-3222
or write TUA at P.O. Box 4000, Dallas TX 75208,
or log on to
TonyEvans.org

ONENESS EMBRACED

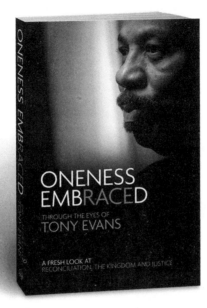

978-0-8024-1790-9

In *Oneness Embraced*, Dr. Evans offers a rare and candid glimpse into the unique backdrop that positioned him as a young theologian between two diverse worlds — that of black, urban culture and white, mainline evangelicalism. Now, three decades later, Evans examines the topics of unity, cultural and church history, the kingdom, social justice, and outreach in this legacy work — giving us a personal look into the nature, purpose and **Power of Oneness**.

Also available as an ebook

MOODY
PUBLISHERS

www.MoodyPublishers.com

THEOLOGY YOU CAN COUNT ON

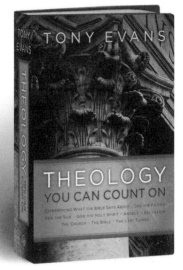

978-0-8024-6653-2

"The Bible is written to real people facing real problems," says Dr. Tony Evans. That's why *Theology You Can Count On* offers theology in bite-size nuggest: short chapters with illustrations that make theology easier to understand. Dr. Evans tackles some of the tough questions. Each chapter ends with personal application as wel as group questions that help you explore the subjects deeper and unlock related Scripture. The book is ideal for private or small-group study.

Also available as an ebook

MOODY
PUBLISHERS

www.MoodyPublishers.com

TONY EVANS'
BOOK OF ILLUSTRATIONS

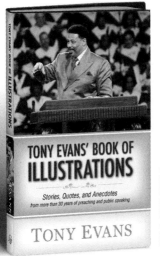

978-0-8024-8578-6

Tony Evans' Book of Illustrations is a collection of stories, quotes, and anecdotes that Tony has gathered over 30 years of preaching and public speaking. These stories are perfect to open a sermon, illustrate a point, or conclude a message. Arranged alphabetically by topic, this book is easy to use and fun to read. From heartwarming stories and personal testimonies to interesting analogies and thought-provoking anecdotes, you'll find everything you need in this valuable resource for ministers and public speakers.

Also available as an ebook

MOODY
PUBLISHERS

www.MoodyPublishers.com